Jordan Blake

Digital Marketing

Dedication by Jordan Blake

To the relentless seekers of knowledge, the innovators embracing change, and the dreamers daring to redefine the future. This book is dedicated to those who navigate the digital landscapes with curiosity, courage, and an unwavering commitment to excellence. May your journey through the digital marketing frontier be as inspiring as the destinations you aim to conquer.

— Jordan Blake

Epigraph by Jordan Blake

"In the vast expanse of digital possibilities, every click is a step into uncharted territories. Navigating the Digital Marketing Frontier isn't just about finding your way—it's about crafting the path to success amidst the ever-evolving landscape. Embrace the journey, embrace the change, and let innovation guide you to new horizons."

— Jordan Blake

Contents

1.

2.

3.

4.

5.

6.

7.

8.

9.

10.

11.

12.

13.

14.

15.

16.

17.

18.

19.

20.

21.

22.

Foreword

Foreword by Jordan Blake

In the ever-evolving landscape of digital marketing, where change is the only constant, "Navigating the Digital Marketing Frontier" emerges as a beacon of guidance. As the author, I've been privileged to witness the transformative power of effective digital strategies and the impact they can have on businesses, big and small.

This book is more than just a compilation of tactics; it's a testament to the dynamic nature of our digital world and the need for marketers to not just keep up but to lead the way. In these pages, you'll discover the keys to unlocking ethical practices, leveraging emerging technologies responsibly, and fostering collaboration across departments for unparalleled success.

As we explore the nuances of this ever-changing landscape, my hope is that you find inspiration, insights, and practical strategies that empower you in your digital marketing endeavors. Whether you're a seasoned professional or someone just starting their journey, this book is crafted with you in mind—a guide to not only surviving but thriving amidst the challenges and opportunities of digital marketing.

So, dive in with curiosity, embrace the challenges, and let the knowledge within these pages be your compass in navigating the vast and exciting digital marketing frontier.

Jordan   Blake

Preface

Preface by Jordan Blake

Welcome to the dynamic realm of digital marketing! As the digital landscape continues to evolve at a breathtaking pace, it's my pleasure to guide you through the intricacies and opportunities that define this frontier. In "Navigating the Digital Marketing Frontier," we embark on a journey of exploration, learning, and strategic mastery.

In a world where trends shift like sand beneath our feet, understanding the core principles of ethical digital marketing is paramount. This book is more than just a guide; it's a compass, steering you through the complexities with a focus on responsible practices and transparent strategies. As we delve into emerging technologies, cross-functional collaboration, and the ever-important human element, you'll find a roadmap to not just survive but thrive in this ever-evolving landscape.

Join me as we uncover the secrets to crafting compelling campaigns, building meaningful relationships with clients, and embracing the technologies that shape the future.

Whether you're a seasoned marketer seeking fresh insights or a newcomer eager to navigate this fascinating frontier, this book is designed to be your companion in the quest for digital marketing excellence.

Let's embark on this journey together, where innovation meets integrity, and where the limitless possibilities of digital marketing unfold before us. Get ready to navigate, adapt, and conquer the digital marketing frontier like never before.

Jordan   Blake

Acknowledgement

Acknowledgments by Jordan Blake

Embarking on the journey to create "Navigating the Digital Marketing Frontier" has been an exhilarating expedition, and no voyage is undertaken alone. As I pen down these acknowledgments, I am filled with gratitude for the incredible individuals and experiences that have shaped this endeavor.

To the brilliant minds and trailblazers in the digital marketing industry, your insights and innovations have been a wellspring of inspiration. Your dedication to pushing the boundaries has motivated me to explore the frontiers of this ever-evolving landscape.

A heartfelt thank you to the readers—both seasoned marketers seeking fresh perspectives and eager newcomers navigating this digital terrain. Your curiosity and enthusiasm for learning fuel the essence of this book.

I extend my deepest gratitude to the teams and collaborators who have contributed their expertise and passion. Your collective efforts have added layers of richness to the fabric of this work.

To my mentors and guides, thank you for your wisdom, guidance, and unwavering support. Your influence has been instrumental in shaping not only the content of this book but also the perspective from which it is presented.

Last but certainly not least, to my family and friends—your encouragement, understanding, and patience during this creative journey have been my pillars of strength.

This book stands as a testament to the power of collaboration, learning, and the shared pursuit of knowledge. Thank you to everyone who has played a part in bringing "Navigating the Digital Marketing Frontier" to life.

With gratitude,

Jordan   Blake

1

Staying informed in digital marketing:

For staying informed in digital marketing:

1. Follow Industry Blogs: Regularly read blogs from reputable sources like Moz, HubSpot, and Neil Patel to stay updated on the latest trends and best practices.

2. Online Courses: Enroll in online courses on platforms like Coursera, LinkedIn Learning, or HubSpot Academy to deepen your knowledge.

3. Podcasts: Listen to digital marketing podcasts to gain insights from industry experts and learn about emerging trends during your commute or downtime.

4. Webinars: Attend webinars hosted by industry leaders and organizations to get firsthand knowledge and engage in Q&A sessions.

5. Social Media Monitoring: Follow industry influencers and participate in discussions on platforms like Twitter and LinkedIn to stay connected and informed.

6. Newsletters: Subscribe to newsletters from marketing platforms and thought leaders to receive curated content and updates directly in your inbox.

7. Conferences and Events: Attend digital marketing conferences and events to network, learn from experts, and discover new tools and strategies.

8. Google Alerts: Set up Google Alerts for relevant keywords and industry terms to receive notifications about the latest news and articles.

9. Join Online Communities: Participate in forums and online communities like Reddit or specialized marketing groups to discuss trends and share insights with peers.

10. Read Industry Reports: Explore industry reports and studies from reputable organizations to gain a deeper understanding of market trends and consumer behavior.

2

Mastering data analysis in digital marketing

For mastering data analysis in digital marketing:

1. Google Analytics Basics: Understand the fundamentals of Google Analytics, including setting up an account, creating goals, and interpreting key metrics.

2. Conversion Tracking: Implement conversion tracking to measure the success of specific actions on your website, such as form submissions or product purchases.

3. Custom Reports: Learn how to create custom reports in Google Analytics to tailor data analysis to your specific business goals.

4. Google Tag Manager: Familiarize yourself with Google Tag Manager to efficiently manage and deploy tracking codes without relying on web developers.

5. Social Media Analytics: Explore the analytics tools provided by social media platforms (e.g., Facebook Insights, Twitter Analytics) to assess the performance of your social campaigns.

6. Heatmaps and Click Tracking: Use tools like Hotjar or Crazy Egg to analyze user behavior through heatmaps and click tracking, helping you understand how visitors interact with your site.

7. A/B Testing Tools: Implement A/B testing using tools like Optimizely or Google Optimize to experiment with different elements and determine what resonates best with your audience.

8. Attribution Modeling: Understand different attribution models (first-click, last-click, multi-touch) to evaluate the impact of various touchpoints in the customer journey.

9. Excel/Google Sheets Skills: Enhance your spreadsheet skills to manipulate and analyze data effectively, as this is crucial for in-depth data analysis.

10. Learn SQL: Basic knowledge of SQL can be valuable for extracting and manipulating data directly from databases, enhancing your ability to work with large datasets.

11. Data Visualization: Master tools like Tableau or Google Data Studio to create visually appealing and informative reports for stakeholders.

12. Regular Monitoring: Set up regular monitoring routines to track key performance indicators (KPIs) and promptly identify any trends or anomalies.

13. Google Search Console: Utilize Google Search Console to understand how your site performs in search results and identify opportunities for improvement.

14. E-commerce Analytics: If applicable, delve into e-commerce analytics platforms (e.g., Shopify Analytics, Magento Analytics) to optimize online store performance.

15. Continuous Learning: Stay updated on new analytics tools and features by exploring online resources, attending webinars, and participating in relevant forums.

3

Creating high-quality and relevant content in digital marketing:

For creating high-quality and relevant content in digital marketing:

1. Know Your Audience: Understand your target audience's demographics, interests, and pain points to tailor your content to their needs.

2. Keyword Research: Conduct thorough keyword research using tools like Google Keyword Planner or SEMrush to identify relevant topics and optimize for search engines.

3. Content Calendar: Develop a content calendar to plan and organize your content creation efforts, ensuring consistency and relevance.

4. Compelling Headlines: Craft attention-grabbing headlines that entice users to click and engage with your content.

5. Storytelling: Incorporate storytelling elements to make your content more relatable and memorable for your audience.

6. Visual Appeal: Use high-quality images, infographics, and videos to enhance the visual appeal of your content and keep your audience engaged.

7. SEO Best Practices: Optimize your content for search engines by incorporating relevant keywords, meta tags, and creating SEO-friendly URLs.

8. Originality: Strive for originality in your content to set yourself apart from competitors and provide unique value to your audience.

9. Clear Structure: Organize your content with a clear and logical structure, including headings, subheadings, and bullet points for easy readability.

10. Audience Engagement: Encourage audience engagement through comments, social shares, and interactive elements like polls or quizzes.

11. Content-Length Variation: Experiment with different content lengths (short-form and long-form) based on the topic and audience preferences.

12. Mobile Optimization: Ensure that your content is mobile-friendly, considering the increasing number of users accessing content on smartphones and tablets.

13. User-Generated Content: Encourage your audience to create and share content related to your brand, fostering a sense of community and authenticity.

14. Research Competitors: Analyze your competitors' content strategies to identify opportunities and ensure your content stands out in the industry.

15. Calls-to-Action (CTAs): Include clear and compelling CTAs to guide your audience towards desired actions, whether it's making a purchase or subscribing to your newsletter.

16. Regular Updates: Keep your content up-to-date by revisiting and refreshing older pieces to maintain relevance and accuracy.

17. Feedback Integration: Pay attention to audience feedback and comments to understand what resonates and adjust your content strategy accordingly.

18. Multichannel Distribution: Distribute your content across various channels, including social media, email, and third-party platforms, to reach a broader audience.

19. Analytics Tracking: Utilize analytics tools to track the performance of your content and refine your strategy based on user behavior and engagement metrics.

20. Continuous Improvement: Stay agile and continuously improve your content strategy based on evolving trends, audience feedback, and performance metrics.

4

Understanding and implementing effective Search Engine Optimization (SEO) strategies in digital marketing:

For understanding and implementing effective Search Engine Optimization (SEO) strategies in digital marketing:

1. Keyword Research: Begin with thorough keyword research to identify relevant terms and phrases your audience is searching for. Use tools like Google Keyword Planner, SEMrush, or Ahrefs.

2. On-Page Optimization: Optimize individual pages by incorporating target keywords in meta titles, meta descriptions, headers, and throughout the content. Ensure a natural and user-friendly approach.

3. Quality Content: Create high-quality, valuable, and relevant content that satisfies user intent. Search engines prioritize content that answers users' questions and provides a positive user experience.

4. Mobile-Friendly Design: Ensure your website is mobile-friendly, as Google considers mobile compatibility when ranking sites. Use responsive design and test your site's mobile performance regularly.

5. Page Speed Optimization: Improve page loading times by optimizing images, using browser caching, and employing Content Delivery Networks (CDNs) to enhance user experience and search rankings.

6. User Experience (UX): Prioritize user experience by having a clear site structure, easy navigation, and engaging, readable content. A positive user experience contributes to better SEO rankings.

7. Backlink Building: Build high-quality backlinks from reputable and relevant websites. Focus on earning links naturally through valuable content rather than using black-hat SEO tactics.

8. Technical SEO: Address technical aspects such as XML sitemaps, robots.txt files, and canonical tags to ensure search engines can crawl and index your site effectively.

9. Local SEO: If applicable, optimize for local search by claiming your Google My Business listing, ensuring consistent NAP (Name, Address, Phone) information, and obtaining positive local reviews.

10. Schema Markup: Implement schema markup to provide search engines with additional context about your content, enhancing the chances of rich snippets appearing in search results.

11. Regular Content Updates: Keep your content fresh and relevant. Regularly update and repurpose existing content to show search engines that your site provides up-to-date and valuable information.

12. Social Signals: While not a direct ranking factor, social signals can indirectly impact SEO. Encourage social sharing and engagement to enhance your content's visibility.

13. Monitor Analytics: Use tools like Google Analytics and Google Search Console to monitor site performance, track user behavior, and identify areas for improvement.

14. Competitor Analysis: Analyze competitors to identify strengths and weaknesses in their SEO strategies, gaining insights to refine your own approach.

15. Voice Search Optimization: Adapt your content for voice search by focusing on natural language and long-tail keywords that match conversational queries.

16. Secure Website (HTTPS): Ensure your website is secure with HTTPS, as Google considers secure sites more trustworthy and may give them a slight ranking boost.

17. Local Citations: If applicable, ensure your business information is consistent across online directories and platforms, contributing to local SEO efforts.

18. User Intent Understanding: Align your content with user intent. Understand the different types of search intent

(informational, navigational, transactional) and tailor your content accordingly.

19. Influencer Collaboration: Collaborate with influencers in your industry to earn quality backlinks and increase your brand's visibility.

20. Adapt to Algorithm Changes: Stay informed about search engine algorithm updates and be ready to adapt your SEO strategy accordingly to maintain and improve rankings.

5

Fostering engagement on social media platforms in digital marketing:

For fostering engagement on social media platforms in digital marketing:

1. Platform Selection: Identify the social media platforms most relevant to your target audience. Focus on platforms where your audience is most active.

2. Consistent Branding: Maintain consistent branding across all social media profiles, including profile pictures, cover images, and bio information.

3. Content Variety: Diversify your content types, including images, videos, infographics, and text posts, to cater to different audience preferences.

4. Content Calendar: Plan and schedule your social media content in advance using a content calendar. This ensures a consistent and organized posting schedule.

5. Audience Engagement: Respond promptly to comments, messages, and mentions. Actively engage with your audience by asking questions, running polls, and encouraging discussions.

6. Use of Hashtags: Research and use relevant hashtags to increase the discoverability of your content. Create branded hashtags to encourage user-generated content.

7. Visual Appeal: Invest in visually appealing and high-quality visuals. Eye-catching images and videos are more likely to grab attention in crowded social media feeds.

8. Timing Matters: Post content when your target audience is most active. Use social media analytics tools to determine the optimal posting times for each platform.

9. Live Video: Embrace live video streaming to connect with your audience in real-time. Live sessions create a sense of urgency and encourage immediate engagement.

10. Collaborations: Collaborate with influencers, other brands, or industry experts to expand your reach and tap into new audience segments.

11. Contests and Giveaways: Run contests or giveaways to encourage participation and generate excitement among your followers.

12. Personalized Content: Tailor your content to the interests and preferences of your audience. Showcasing authenticity and a personal touch can enhance engagement.

13. Community Building: Foster a sense of community among your followers. Encourage them to share their experiences, opinions, and content related to your brand.

14.Analytics Monitoring: Use analytics tools provided by social media platforms or third-party tools to track performance metrics. Analyze engagement data and adjust your strategy accordingly.

15. Paid Advertising: Utilize paid advertising options on social media platforms to amplify your reach and target specific demographics.

16. Social Media Listening: Monitor social media for mentions of your brand, industry trends, and customer feedback. Use this information to adapt your strategy and address concerns.

17. Story Features: Make use of story features on platforms like Instagram, Facebook, and Snapchat to share behind-the-scenes content and time-sensitive updates.

18. Educational Content: Share valuable and educational content to position your brand as an authority in your industry. How-to guides, tips, and tutorials can be particularly effective.

19. Cross-Promotion: Cross-promote content across different social media channels to maximize visibility and reach a broader audience.

20. Adapt to Algorithm Changes: Stay informed about changes in social media algorithms and adjust your strategy to ensure your content remains visible to your audience.

6

Developing targeted and personalized email campaigns in digital marketing:

For developing targeted and personalized email campaigns in digital marketing:

1. Segment Your Audience: Divide your email list into segments based on demographics, preferences, or behaviors to send more targeted and relevant content.

2. Build a Quality Email List: Focus on growing a quality email list with engaged and interested subscribers. Avoid purchasing email lists to ensure better deliverability and engagement.

3. Personalization: Use personalization tokens to address subscribers by their name and customize content based on their preferences or previous interactions.

4. Compelling Subject Lines: Craft compelling and concise subject lines that grab attention and entice recipients to open your emails.

5. Clear Call-to-Action (CTA): Clearly define the purpose of your email and include a prominent and compelling CTA to guide recipients toward the desired action.

6. Responsive Design: Ensure your email templates are mobile-friendly and display well on various devices. Many users check emails on smartphones, so a responsive design is crucial.

7. A/B Testing: Experiment with different elements of your emails, such as subject lines, CTAs, or visuals, using A/B testing to identify what resonates best with your audience.

8. Timing and Frequency: Test different send times and frequencies to determine when your audience is most responsive. Avoid overwhelming subscribers with excessive emails.

9. Valuable Content: Provide valuable and relevant content in your emails. Whether it's informative articles, special offers, or exclusive insights, make sure it adds value to your subscribers.

10. Automation: Implement automated email campaigns, such as welcome series, drip campaigns, or abandoned cart emails, to streamline communication based on user behavior.

11. Personalized Recommendations: If applicable, include personalized product or content recommendations based on the recipient's past interactions or purchase history.

12. Interactive Elements: Incorporate interactive elements like polls, surveys, or clickable images to encourage engagement and feedback.

13. Email Analytics: Utilize email analytics to track open rates, click-through rates, and other relevant metrics. Analyze the data to refine your future campaigns.

14. Optimize for Deliverability: Ensure your emails reach the inbox by following best practices for email deliverability, including using a reputable email service provider and avoiding spam triggers.

15. Clear Unsubscribe Option: Make it easy for subscribers to opt-out if they choose to. Providing a clear and accessible unsubscribe option builds trust and complies with regulations.

16. Personal Branding: Maintain a consistent brand voice and visual identity across your email campaigns to reinforce brand recognition.

17. Customer Segmentation: Further refine your segments based on customer behavior, such as frequent purchasers, inactive subscribers, or new leads, to tailor your messaging effectively.

18. Urgency and Scarcity: Use psychological triggers like urgency and scarcity to create a sense of importance and drive immediate action.

19. Feedback Solicitation: Encourage feedback from subscribers through surveys or direct replies. Use this feedback to improve your email strategy and better cater to your audience.

20.Compliance with Regulations: Stay informed about email marketing regulations, such as GDPR and CAN-SPAM, to ensure compliance and build trust with your audience.

7

Staying flexible and adapting to changes in algorithms, platforms, and consumer behavior in digital marketing:

For staying flexible and adapting to changes in algorithms, platforms, and consumer behavior in digital marketing:

1. Continuous Learning: Develop a mindset of continuous learning to stay updated on industry trends, algorithm changes, and emerging technologies.

2. Industry News Sources: Follow reputable industry news sources, blogs, and publications to receive timely updates on changes in digital marketing landscape.

3. Webinars and Conferences: Attend webinars and conferences regularly to gain insights from industry experts and network with professionals in your field.

4. Experimentation: Be open to experimentation in your marketing strategies. Test new ideas, formats, and channels to discover what resonates best with your audience.

5. Data Analysis: Regularly analyze data from your campaigns to identify patterns, trends, and areas for improvement. Use data-driven insights to refine your strategies.

6.Customer Feedback: Pay attention to customer feedback through reviews, surveys, and social media. Use this feedback to adapt your approach and address customer concerns.

7. Platform Updates: Stay informed about updates and changes on major digital platforms (Google, Facebook, Twitter, etc.). Understand how these changes may impact your marketing efforts.

8. Adapt to Consumer Behavior: Monitor changes in consumer behavior and adjust your marketing strategies

accordingly. Understand how your audience prefers to engage with content and adapt your channels accordingly.

9. Agile Marketing: Embrace agile marketing methodologies to quickly respond to market changes. This involves iterative planning, testing, and adjusting based on performance.

10. Competitor Analysis: Regularly analyze your competitors to understand their strategies, successes, and failures. Learn from their experiences and adapt your approach accordingly.

11. Social Listening: Use social listening tools to monitor conversations about your brand and industry on social media. Gain insights into consumer sentiment and adjust your messaging as needed.

12. Emerging Technologies: Keep an eye on emerging technologies such as artificial intelligence, augmented reality, or voice search. Evaluate how these technologies can be integrated into your marketing strategies.

13. Customer Personas Update: Regularly update your customer personas based on changes in market dynamics and consumer preferences. This ensures your targeting remains relevant.

14. Crisis Management: Develop a crisis management plan to address unexpected challenges. Be prepared to adapt your messaging and strategies during crises to maintain brand reputation.

15. Cross-Functional Collaboration: Foster collaboration between different departments within your organization. Align marketing efforts with sales, customer service, and product development to adapt to changing business needs.

16. Global and Cultural Awareness: If operating in multiple regions, be culturally sensitive and aware of global trends. Adapt your messaging to resonate with diverse audiences.

17. Review and Reflect: Regularly review and reflect on the performance of your campaigns. Identify successes and areas for improvement, and use these insights to refine your strategies.

18. Networking: Build a strong professional network within the industry. Engage with peers, attend networking events, and participate in forums to stay connected and informed.

19. Regulatory Compliance: Stay updated on regulatory changes in the digital marketing landscape. Comply with

privacy laws and regulations to avoid legal issues and maintain consumer trust.

20. Scenario Planning: Develop scenario planning strategies to anticipate potential changes or disruptions in the market. This proactive approach allows you to be prepared for various   outcomes.

8

Effectively managing your digital marketing budget:

For effectively managing your digital marketing budget:

1. Set Clear Objectives: Clearly define your marketing objectives and goals to guide budget allocation. Whether it's brand awareness, lead generation, or sales, having a clear direction is crucial.

2. Understand Your Audience: Know your target audience's behavior and preferences. This understanding helps optimize budget distribution to channels that resonate most with your audience.

3. Allocate Based on ROI: Prioritize channels and campaigns with the highest return on investment (ROI). Regularly assess and adjust budget allocation based on performance metrics.

4. Experiment with Channels: Allocate a portion of your budget for experimenting with new channels or strategies. This allows you to discover untapped opportunities and diversify your marketing mix.

5. Seasonal Adjustments: Consider seasonal trends that may impact your business. Adjust your budget accordingly to capitalize on peak seasons or allocate resources more efficiently during slower periods.

6. Budget Tracking: Implement robust budget tracking mechanisms. Use tools or software to monitor spending and ensure you stay within allocated limits for each campaign or channel.

7. Performance Metrics: Establish key performance indicators (KPIs) for each campaign or channel. Regularly analyze performance metrics to gauge effectiveness and make informed decisions.

8. Flexible Budgeting: Be flexible with your budget. Market conditions and consumer behaviors can change, requiring adjustments to your budget allocation for optimal results.

9. Benchmarking: Benchmark your budget against industry standards and competitors. This provides insights into

whether your spending aligns with market expectations and helps identify areas for improvement.

10. Negotiate Vendor Contracts: Negotiate favorable terms with vendors, agencies, or platforms. Explore discounts, incentives, or flexible payment options to maximize the value of your budget.

11. Focus on High-Value Audiences: Identify and prioritize high-value customer segments. Allocate a proportionate budget to target and engage these audiences effectively.

12. Content Efficiency: Invest in evergreen and reusable content that provides long-term value. This minimizes the need for constant content creation and optimizes your content-related expenses.

13. Testing and Optimization: Allocate budget for A/B testing and continuous optimization. This ensures that you refine your strategies based on real-time performance data.

14. Customer Lifetime Value (CLV): Consider the lifetime value of your customers when allocating budget. Understanding the long-term impact of your marketing efforts helps justify spending.

15. Emerging Technologies: Set aside a portion of your budget for exploring and adopting emerging technologies. Staying ahead in technology can provide a competitive edge.

16. Contingency Fund: Establish a contingency fund for unforeseen circumstances or opportunities. Having flexibility in your budget allows you to adapt to unexpected changes.

17. Educational Resources: Allocate budget for ongoing training and education for your marketing team. Ensuring that your team is well-equipped with the latest skills can enhance campaign efficiency.

18. Monitor Trends: Keep an eye on industry trends and consumer behavior. Allocate budget to capitalize on emerging trends or adjust your strategy in response to changing market dynamics.

19. Customer Feedback Integration: Use customer feedback to refine your marketing approach. Allocate budget for surveys, feedback mechanisms, or customer support enhancements based on feedback insights.

20. Regular Audits: Conduct regular budget audits to assess the efficiency and effectiveness of your spending. Identify

areas where adjustments can be made to optimize your
overall marketing strategy.

9

Fostering collaboration between different departments in digital marketing:

For fostering collaboration between different departments in digital marketing:

1.Establish Clear Communication Channels: Set up clear and open communication channels between marketing, sales, product development, and customer service teams. Regular communication is essential for collaboration.

2. Shared Goals and Objectives: Ensure that teams across departments share common goals and objectives. This alignment fosters a collaborative mindset focused on overall business success.

3. Cross-Functional Meetings: Schedule regular cross-functional meetings where representatives from different departments can discuss ongoing projects, share insights, and coordinate efforts.

4. Collaboration Tools: Implement collaboration tools such as project management platforms, communication apps, and shared documents to facilitate seamless information exchange and project tracking.

5. Define Roles and Responsibilities: Clearly define roles and responsibilities for each department. This helps avoid misunderstandings and ensures everyone understands their contribution to shared goals.

6. Joint Planning Sessions: Conduct joint planning sessions where representatives from marketing, sales, and product teams collaborate on upcoming campaigns or product launches. This ensures alignment from the early stages.

7. Integrated Data Sharing: Foster a culture of data sharing between departments. Marketing can provide valuable customer insights to product development, and sales can share feedback that informs marketing strategies.

8. Training Workshops: Organize workshops or training sessions where team members from different departments can learn about each other's roles and responsibilities. This builds mutual understanding and appreciation.

9. Cross-Departmental Projects: Encourage collaboration through cross-departmental projects. This not only enhances teamwork but also allows each department to leverage the expertise of others.

10. Feedback Loops: Establish feedback loops between departments. Regularly gather feedback on processes, campaigns, and collaborations to identify areas for improvement.

11. Joint Metrics and KPIs: Define joint metrics and key performance indicators (KPIs) that align with overall business objectives. This ensures that everyone is working towards common goals.

12. Team Building Activities: Organize team-building activities or events to strengthen interpersonal relationships. A positive and collaborative work environment fosters better cooperation.

13. Regular Updates:Keep teams informed about each other's activities through regular updates. This transparency ensures that everyone is aware of ongoing projects and can provide valuable input.

14. Inclusive Decision-Making: Involve representatives from different departments in decision-making processes. This inclusivity promotes a sense of ownership and commitment to shared initiatives.

15. Conflict Resolution Protocols: Establish protocols for resolving conflicts that may arise between departments. An effective resolution process ensures that collaboration continues smoothly.

16. Shared Resources: Pool resources such as data, tools, or expertise to maximize efficiency. Shared resources can lead to cost savings and improved outcomes for joint projects.

17. Recognition and Rewards: Acknowledge and reward cross-departmental collaboration. Recognition programs motivate teams and individuals to actively engage in collaborative efforts.

18. Cross-Training Opportunities: Provide opportunities for cross-training between departments. This enables team

members to gain insights into different functions and promotes a holistic understanding of the business.

19. Regular Performance Reviews: Include collaborative efforts in performance reviews. Recognize and evaluate contributions to cross-departmental projects as part of individual performance assessments.

20. Adaptability: Encourage adaptability to change. In the dynamic business environment, the ability to quickly adapt to new challenges and opportunities is crucial for effective collaboration across departments.

10

Optimizing your digital marketing efforts for mobile users:

For optimizing your digital marketing efforts for mobile users:

1. Responsive Web Design: Ensure your website is designed responsively to provide an optimal viewing and interaction experience across a variety of devices, including smartphones and tablets.

2. Mobile-First Approach: Adopt a mobile-first mindset when designing campaigns and content. Prioritize mobile users in your strategies, considering the limitations and preferences of smaller screens.

3. Page Speed Optimization: Optimize your website's loading speed for mobile devices. Users expect fast load

times, and search engines favor websites that provide a smooth mobile experience.

4. Mobile-Friendly Content: Create content that is easily consumable on mobile devices. Use concise and engaging headlines, break up text with visuals, and ensure readability on smaller screens.

5. Mobile SEO: Implement mobile SEO best practices, such as optimizing meta tags, using mobile-friendly URLs, and ensuring that your site is accessible to search engine crawlers on mobile devices.

6. Mobile App Presence: If applicable, ensure that your brand has a mobile app presence. Optimize the app for usability and provide valuable features to enhance the mobile experience for users.

7. Mobile-Friendly Emails: Design email campaigns with a mobile-friendly layout. Use a single-column design, large buttons, and readable fonts to enhance the mobile email experience.

8. Optimized Forms: If your site includes forms, optimize them for mobile users. Minimize the number of fields, use

dropdowns when possible, and ensure that form submission is straightforward on smaller screens.

9. Location-Based Targeting: Utilize location-based targeting to deliver relevant content or promotions to users based on their geographic location. This enhances the personalization of your mobile marketing efforts.

10. Mobile Payment Options: If applicable to your business, provide mobile-friendly payment options. Ensure that the checkout process is streamlined for users making purchases on their mobile devices.

11. Push Notifications:Implement push notification strategies for mobile apps to engage users with timely updates, promotions, or relevant information.

12. Mobile Analytics: Use mobile analytics tools to gather insights into user behavior on mobile devices. Understand how users interact with your content and optimize accordingly.

13. Voice Search Optimization: Adapt your content for voice search as more users are using voice-activated assistants on their mobile devices. Use conversational keywords and phrases in your content.

14. Mobile-Specific Ad Formats: Utilize mobile-specific ad formats on platforms like Google Ads and social media. These formats are designed to capture the attention of mobile users effectively.

15. Mobile-Friendly Social Media: Ensure that your social media content is optimized for mobile viewing. Use visuals that are easy to see on smaller screens and create concise captions.

16. Progressive Web Apps (PWAs): Consider implementing PWAs to provide a more app-like experience for users accessing your website on mobile browsers.

17. User Testing on Mobile Devices: Conduct user testing specifically on mobile devices to identify any usability issues or areas for improvement in the mobile experience.

18. Mobile-Friendly Customer Support: Provide mobile-friendly customer support options, such as live chat or mobile-responsive contact forms, to assist users on the go.

19. Mobile-Focused Social Media Advertising: Design and optimize your social media ads for mobile platforms. Ensure that visuals and ad copy are compelling and easily digestible on mobile screens.

20. Cross-Device Consistency: Maintain consistency in branding and messaging across all devices. A seamless transition between desktop and mobile experiences enhances user trust and engagement.

11

Effectively implementing Search Engine Optimization (SEO) strategies in digital marketing:

For effectively implementing Search Engine Optimization (SEO) strategies in digital marketing:

1. Keyword Research: Begin with thorough keyword research to identify relevant terms and phrases your audience is searching for. Use tools like Google Keyword Planner, SEMrush, or Ahrefs.

2. On-Page Optimization: Optimize individual pages by incorporating target keywords in meta titles, meta descriptions, headers, and throughout the content. Ensure a natural and user-friendly approach.

3. Quality Content: Create high-quality, valuable, and relevant content that satisfies user intent. Search engines prioritize content that answers users' questions and provides a positive user experience.

4. Mobile-Friendly Design: Ensure your website is mobile-friendly, as Google considers mobile compatibility when ranking sites. Use responsive design and test your site's mobile performance regularly.

5. Page Speed Optimization: Improve page loading times by optimizing images, using browser caching, and employing Content Delivery Networks (CDNs) to enhance user experience and search rankings.

6. User Experience (UX): Prioritize user experience by having a clear site structure, easy navigation, and engaging, readable content. A positive user experience contributes to better SEO rankings.

7. Backlink Building:Build high-quality backlinks from reputable and relevant websites. Focus on earning links naturally through valuable content rather than using black-hat SEO tactics.

8. Technical SEO: Address technical aspects such as XML sitemaps, robots.txt files, and canonical tags to ensure search engines can crawl and index your site effectively.

9. Local SEO: If applicable, optimize for local search by claiming your Google My Business listing, ensuring consistent NAP (Name, Address, Phone) information, and obtaining positive local reviews.

10. Schema Markup: Implement schema markup to provide search engines with additional context about your content, enhancing the chances of rich snippets appearing in search results.

11. Regular Content Updates: Keep your content fresh and relevant. Regularly update and repurpose existing pieces to show search engines that your site provides up-to-date and valuable information.

12. Social Media Integration: Integrate social media into your SEO strategy. Social signals may not be direct ranking factors, but social engagement can indirectly impact your site's visibility.

13. Voice Search Optimization: Adapt your content for voice search by focusing on natural language and long-tail keywords that match conversational queries.

14. Secure Website (HTTPS): Ensure your website is secure with HTTPS, as Google considers secure sites more trustworthy and may give them a slight ranking boost.

15. User-Generated Content: Encourage user-generated content through reviews, comments, and social media interactions. User-generated content can contribute positively to your site's SEO.

16. Local Citations: If applicable, ensure your business information is consistent across online directories and platforms, contributing to local SEO efforts.

17. User Intent Understanding: Align your content with user intent. Understand the different types of search intent (informational, navigational, transactional) and tailor your content accordingly.

18. Content Length Variation: Experiment with different content lengths based on the topic and user intent. Some queries may require in-depth, long-form content, while others may be better suited for shorter pieces.

19. Influencer Collaboration: Collaborate with influencers in your industry to earn quality backlinks and increase your brand's visibility.

20. Adapt to Algorithm Changes: Stay informed about search engine algorithm updates and adjust your SEO strategy accordingly. Flexibility and adaptability are key in the ever-evolving landscape of SEO.

12

Leveraging the power of video marketing in your digital strategy:

For leveraging the power of video marketing in your digital strategy:

1. Define Objectives: Clearly outline your video marketing objectives. Whether it's brand awareness, lead generation, or product promotion, understanding your goals will shape your video content.

2. Understand Your Audience: Know your target audience and create videos that resonate with their interests, preferences, and pain points. Tailoring content to your audience enhances engagement.

3. Quality Production: Invest in high-quality video production. While you don't always need expensive

equipment, ensure your videos have good lighting, clear audio, and a professional appearance.

4. Diverse Video Types: Explore various video formats, including explainer videos, tutorials, product demos, testimonials, and behind-the-scenes footage. Diversifying your content keeps your audience engaged.

5. Optimize for Platforms: Tailor your videos for specific platforms. Each platform (YouTube, Instagram, Facebook, etc.) has different requirements and best practices, so optimize accordingly.

6. Engaging Thumbnails: Create attention-grabbing thumbnails. Thumbnails are the first impression viewers get, and a compelling image can significantly increase click-through rates.

7. Compelling Introductions: Capture attention in the first few seconds. Start your videos with a hook to entice viewers and encourage them to watch the entire content.

8. Storytelling: Incorporate storytelling elements to make your videos more engaging and relatable. Tell a compelling narrative that resonates with your audience.

9. Clear Calls-to-Action (CTAs): Include clear CTAs in your videos. Guide viewers on what action to take next, whether it's visiting your website, subscribing, or making a purchase.

10. Consistent Branding: Maintain consistent branding across your videos. Use consistent visuals, logos, and messaging to reinforce your brand identity.

11. Mobile Optimization: Design videos with mobile users in mind. Ensure that your videos are easily viewable on various devices, especially smartphones.

12. Engage with Comments: Actively engage with comments and feedback on your videos. Responding to viewer comments fosters a sense of community and encourages more interaction.

13. Video SEO: Optimize videos for search engines. Use relevant keywords in video titles, descriptions, and tags to improve discoverability on platforms like YouTube.

14. Collaborations: Collaborate with influencers or other brands to expand your reach. Partnering with others can introduce your videos to new audiences.

15. Live Streaming: Experiment with live streaming. Live videos create a sense of immediacy and allow real-time interaction with your audience.

16. Analytics Monitoring: Use analytics tools provided by platforms to track video performance. Analyze metrics like views, watch time, and audience retention to refine your strategy.

17. Interactive Elements: Incorporate interactive elements like polls, quizzes, or clickable links within your videos to increase viewer engagement.

18. Educational Content: Provide educational value. Whether it's tutorials, how-to guides, or informative content, offering value establishes your brand as an authority in your niche.

19. Closed Captions: Include closed captions in your videos. This enhances accessibility and accommodates viewers who prefer or require captions.

20. Experiment and Iterate: Be willing to experiment with different video styles and content. Analyze performance data and iterate based on what resonates most with your audience.

13

Creating compelling visual content in digital marketing:

For creating compelling visual content in digital marketing:

1. Understand Your Audience: Know your target audience's preferences, interests, and visual style. Tailor your visual content to resonate with your specific demographic.

2. Consistent Branding: Maintain a consistent visual identity across all your marketing materials. This includes using the same color scheme, fonts, and logo to reinforce brand recognition.

3. Quality Imagery: Invest in high-quality images. Whether it's photographs, graphics, or illustrations, visually appealing and professional-quality visuals enhance the overall perception of your brand.

4. Storytelling with Visuals: Use visuals to tell a story. Whether through infographics, slideshows, or sequential images, storytelling adds depth and emotional connection to your content.

5. Visual Hierarchy: Design with a clear visual hierarchy. Guide the viewer's eye through the content with strategic use of color, contrast, and placement to emphasize key elements.

6. Eye-Catching Headlines: Combine strong visuals with compelling headlines. The right combination of visuals and text can grab attention and convey your message effectively.

7. Responsive Design: Ensure that your visual content is optimized for different devices. Responsive design ensures a seamless experience, whether your audience is viewing content on a desktop, tablet, or smartphone.

8.Interactive Visuals: Experiment with interactive visuals. This could include clickable elements, animated graphics, or immersive experiences that engage and involve the audience.

9. Typography Matters: Pay attention to typography in your visual content. Choose fonts that align with your brand and ensure readability, especially when incorporating text into images.

10. Color Psychology: Understand the psychology of colors. Different colors evoke specific emotions and associations, so choose colors that align with your brand personality and the message you want to convey.

11. Use of Negative Space: Embrace negative space in your designs. Sometimes, less is more, and allowing for white space or negative space can enhance clarity and focus.

12. Consistent Image Styles: If using photography, maintain a consistent style. This could involve similar filters, color tones, or compositions to create a cohesive visual theme.

13. Brand Personality: Infuse your visual content with your brand's personality. Whether it's playful, sophisticated, or adventurous, let your visuals reflect the essence of your brand.

14. Visual Storyboarding: Plan your visual content with storyboarding. This involves sketching or planning the sequence of images to ensure a cohesive and effective visual narrative.

15. Cultural Sensitivity: Be culturally sensitive in your visuals. Ensure that your images are respectful and inclusive, considering diverse perspectives and backgrounds.

16. User-Generated Content: Encourage your audience to contribute visual content. User-generated visuals not only provide authenticity but also foster a sense of community around your brand.

17. Test Different Formats: Experiment with different visual formats. This could include image carousels, GIFs, memes, or other formats that align with your brand and engage your audience.

18. Visual Consistency Across Channels: Maintain visual consistency across different marketing channels. Whether on

social media, your website, or email campaigns, a consistent visual style builds brand coherence.

19. Infographics for Complex Information: Use infographics to simplify complex information. Visualizing data or processes in an infographic format makes it easier for your audience to understand and retain information.

20. Accessibility Considerations: Ensure your visual content is accessible to everyone. Provide alternative text for images, use descriptive captions, and design with accessibility in mind to cater to a broader audience.

14

Effective email marketing strategies in digital marketing:

For effective email marketing strategies in digital marketing:

1. Segment Your Email List: Divide your email subscribers into segments based on demographics, behaviors, or preferences. Targeted emails are more likely to resonate with specific audience segments.

2. Personalize Email Content: Personalization goes beyond addressing subscribers by their name. Use data to personalize content based on their previous interactions, purchase history, or preferences.

3. Clear and Compelling Subject Lines: Craft subject lines that are clear, concise, and compelling. Your subject line

should entice recipients to open the email while setting expectations for the content inside.

4. Mobile-Responsive Design: Ensure your emails are mobile-friendly. Many users check their emails on smartphones, so a responsive design is crucial for a positive user experience.

5. A/B Testing: Experiment with A/B testing for different elements of your emails, such as subject lines, sender names, or content variations. Analyze the results to optimize future campaigns.

6. Create Engaging Content: Develop content that is engaging, valuable, and relevant to your audience. This could include informative articles, product updates, promotions, or exclusive offers.

7. Use of Visuals: Incorporate visually appealing elements in your emails. This could be images, infographics, or videos to make your content more attractive and shareable.

8. Clear Call-to-Action (CTA): Clearly define the purpose of your email and include a compelling CTA. Whether it's making a purchase, signing up, or clicking through to your website, guide recipients on the desired action.

9. Timing Matters: Experiment with the timing of your emails. Test different days and times to identify when your audience is most responsive. Consider time zones and the nature of your content.

10. Automated Email Campaigns: Implement automated email campaigns for various scenarios such as welcome emails, abandoned cart reminders, or post-purchase follow-ups. Automation streamlines communication based on user behavior.

11. Segmented Email Funnels: Create segmented email funnels based on user behavior. Tailor your email sequences to guide subscribers through the customer journey, providing relevant content at each stage.

12. Social Proof: Incorporate social proof in your emails. This could be customer reviews, testimonials, or user-generated content that adds credibility and encourages trust.

13. Email Analytics: Regularly analyze email performance metrics such as open rates, click-through rates, and conversion rates. Use this data to understand what works and refine your email strategy.

14. Personalized Recommendations: If applicable, include personalized product or content recommendations based on the recipient's previous interactions or purchase history.

15. Feedback and Surveys: Gather feedback from your email subscribers. This could be through surveys or direct requests for input, helping you understand their preferences and improve your email content.

16. Subscription Preferences: Allow subscribers to manage their subscription preferences. Giving them control over the type and frequency of emails they receive improves satisfaction and reduces the likelihood of unsubscribing.

17. Optimize Email Deliverability: Monitor and optimize for email deliverability. Ensure that your emails land in the inbox rather than the spam folder by following best practices and maintaining a clean email list.

18. Engagement-Based Segmentation: Segment your list based on engagement levels. Identify and re-engage inactive

subscribers with targeted campaigns to revive their interest in your brand.

19. Transactional Emails: Enhance transactional emails. Confirmation emails, receipts, and shipping notifications provide additional opportunities to engage customers and encourage further interaction.

20. Compliance with Regulations: Stay informed about email marketing regulations such as GDPR and CAN-SPAM. Ensure your email campaigns comply with these regulations to build trust and avoid legal issues.

15

Staying flexible and adapting to changes in algorithms, platforms, and consumer behavior in digital marketing:

For staying flexible and adapting to changes in algorithms, platforms, and consumer behavior in digital marketing:

1. Continuous Learning: Develop a mindset of continuous learning to stay updated on industry trends, algorithm changes, and emerging technologies.

2. Industry News Sources: Follow reputable industry news sources, blogs, and publications to receive timely updates on changes in the digital marketing landscape.

3. Webinars and Conferences: Attend webinars and conferences regularly to gain insights from industry experts and network with professionals in your field.

4. Experimentation: Be open to experimentation in your marketing strategies. Test new ideas, formats, and channels to discover what resonates best with your audience.

5. Data Analysis: Regularly analyze data from your campaigns to identify patterns, trends, and areas for improvement. Use data-driven insights to refine your strategies.

6. Customer Feedback: Pay attention to customer feedback through reviews, surveys, and social media. Use this feedback to adapt your approach and address customer concerns.

7. Platform Updates: Stay informed about updates and changes on major digital platforms (Google, Facebook, Twitter, etc.). Understand how these changes may impact your marketing efforts.

8. Adapt to Consumer Behavior: Monitor changes in consumer behavior and adjust your marketing strategies

accordingly. Understand how your audience prefers to engage with content and adapt your channels accordingly.

9. Agile Marketing: Embrace agile marketing methodologies to quickly respond to market changes. This involves iterative planning, testing, and adjusting based on performance.

10.Competitor Analysis: Regularly analyze your competitors to understand their strategies, successes, and failures. Learn from their experiences and adapt your approach accordingly.

11. Social Listening: Use social listening tools to monitor conversations about your brand and industry on social media. Gain insights into consumer sentiment and adjust your messaging as needed.

12. Emerging Technologies: Keep an eye on emerging technologies such as artificial intelligence, augmented reality, or voice search. Evaluate how these technologies can be integrated into your marketing strategies.

13. Customer Personas Update: Regularly update your customer personas based on changes in market dynamics and consumer preferences. This ensures your targeting remains relevant.

14. Crisis Management: Develop a crisis management plan to address unexpected challenges. Be prepared to adapt your messaging and strategies during crises to maintain brand reputation.

15. Cross-Functional Collaboration: Foster collaboration between different departments within your organization. Align marketing efforts with sales, customer service, and product development to adapt to changing business needs.

16. Global and Cultural Awareness: If operating in multiple regions, be culturally sensitive and aware of global trends. Adapt your messaging to resonate with diverse audiences.

17. Review and Reflect: Regularly review and reflect on the performance of your campaigns. Identify successes and areas for improvement, and use these insights to refine your strategies.

18. Networking: Build a strong professional network within the industry. Engage with peers, attend networking events, and participate in forums to stay connected and informed.

19. Regulatory Compliance: Stay updated on regulatory changes in the digital marketing landscape. Comply with

privacy laws and regulations to ensure compliance and build trust with your audience.

20. Scenario Planning: Develop scenario planning strategies to anticipate potential changes or disruptions in the market. This proactive approach allows you to be prepared for various   outcomes.

16

Effectively managing your digital marketing budget:

For effectively managing your digital marketing budget:

1. Set Clear Objectives: Clearly define your marketing objectives and goals to guide budget allocation. Whether it's brand awareness, lead generation, or sales, having a clear direction is crucial.

2. Understand Your Audience: Know your target audience's behavior and preferences. This understanding helps optimize budget distribution to channels that resonate most with your audience.

3. Allocate Based on ROI: Prioritize channels and campaigns with the highest return on investment (ROI). Regularly assess and adjust budget allocation based on performance metrics.

4. Experiment with Channels: Allocate a portion of your budget for experimenting with new channels or strategies. This allows you to discover untapped opportunities and diversify your marketing mix.

5. Seasonal Adjustments: Consider seasonal trends that may impact your business. Adjust your budget accordingly to capitalize on peak seasons or allocate resources more efficiently during slower periods.

6. Budget Tracking: Implement robust budget tracking mechanisms. Use tools or software to monitor spending and ensure you stay within allocated limits for each campaign or channel.

7. Performance Metrics: Establish key performance indicators (KPIs) for each campaign or channel. Regularly analyze performance metrics to gauge effectiveness and make informed decisions.

8. Flexible Budgeting: Be flexible with your budget. Market conditions and consumer behaviors can change, requiring adjustments to your budget allocation for optimal results.

9. Benchmarking: Benchmark your budget against industry standards and competitors. This provides insights into

whether your spending aligns with market expectations and helps identify areas for improvement.

10. Negotiate Vendor Contracts: Negotiate favorable terms with vendors, agencies, or platforms. Explore discounts, incentives, or flexible payment options to maximize the value of your budget.

11. Focus on High-Value Audiences: Identify and prioritize high-value customer segments. Allocate a proportionate budget to target and engage these audiences effectively.

12. Content Efficiency: Invest in evergreen and reusable content that provides long-term value. This minimizes the need for constant content creation and optimizes your content-related expenses.

13. Testing and Optimization: Allocate budget for A/B testing and continuous optimization. This ensures that you refine your strategies based on real-time performance data.

14. Customer Lifetime Value (CLV): Consider the lifetime value of your customers when allocating budget. Understanding the long-term impact of your marketing efforts helps justify spending.

15. Emerging Technologies: Set aside a portion of your budget for exploring and adopting emerging technologies. Staying ahead in technology can provide a competitive edge.

16. Contingency Fund: Establish a contingency fund for unforeseen circumstances or opportunities. Having flexibility in your budget allows you to adapt to unexpected changes.

17. Educational Resources: Allocate budget for ongoing training and education for your marketing team. Ensuring that your team is well-equipped with the latest skills can enhance campaign efficiency.

18. Monitor Trends: Keep an eye on industry trends and consumer behavior. Allocate budget to capitalize on emerging trends or adjust your strategy in response to changing market dynamics.

19. Customer Feedback Integration: Use customer feedback to refine your marketing approach. Allocate budget for surveys, feedback mechanisms, or customer support enhancements based on feedback insights.

20. Regular Audits: Conduct regular budget audits to assess the efficiency and effectiveness of your spending. Identify

areas where adjustments can be made to optimize your overall marketing strategy.

17

Fostering collaboration between different departments in digital marketing:

For fostering collaboration between different departments in digital marketing:

1. Establish Clear Communication Channels: Set up clear and open communication channels between marketing, sales, product development, and customer service teams. Regular communication is essential for collaboration.

2. Shared Goals and Objectives: Ensure that teams across departments share common goals and objectives. This alignment fosters a collaborative mindset focused on overall business success.

3. Cross-Functional Meetings: Schedule regular cross-functional meetings where representatives from different departments can discuss ongoing projects, share insights, and coordinate efforts.

4. Collaboration Tools: Implement collaboration tools such as project management platforms, communication apps, and shared documents to facilitate seamless information exchange and project tracking.

5. Define Roles and Responsibilities: Clearly define roles and responsibilities for each department. This helps avoid misunderstandings and ensures everyone understands their contribution to shared goals.

6. Joint Planning Sessions: Conduct joint planning sessions where representatives from marketing, sales, and product teams collaborate on upcoming campaigns or product launches. This ensures alignment from the early stages.

7. Integrated Data Sharing: Foster a culture of data sharing between departments. Marketing can provide valuable customer insights to product development, and sales can share feedback that informs marketing strategies.

8. Training Workshops: Organize workshops or training sessions where team members from different departments can learn about each other's roles and responsibilities. This builds mutual understanding and appreciation.

9. Cross-Departmental Projects: Encourage collaboration through cross-departmental projects. This not only enhances teamwork but also allows each department to leverage the expertise of others.

10. Feedback Loops: Establish feedback loops between departments. Regularly gather feedback on processes, campaigns, and collaborations to identify areas for improvement.

11. Joint Metrics and KPIs: Define joint metrics and key performance indicators (KPIs) that align with overall business objectives. This ensures that everyone is working towards common goals.

12. Team Building Activities: Organize team-building activities or events to strengthen interpersonal relationships. A positive and collaborative work environment fosters better cooperation.

13. Regular Updates: Keep teams informed about each other's activities through regular updates. This transparency ensures that everyone is aware of ongoing projects and can provide valuable input.

14. Inclusive Decision-Making: Involve representatives from different departments in decision-making processes. This inclusivity promotes a sense of ownership and commitment to shared initiatives.

15. Conflict Resolution Protocols: Establish protocols for resolving conflicts that may arise between departments. An effective resolution process ensures that collaboration continues smoothly.

16. Shared Resources: Pool resources such as data, tools, or expertise to maximize efficiency. Shared resources can lead to cost savings and improved outcomes for joint projects.

17. Recognition and Rewards: Acknowledge and reward cross-departmental collaboration. Recognition programs motivate teams and individuals to actively engage in collaborative efforts.

18. Cross-Training Opportunities: Provide opportunities for cross-training between departments. This enables team

members to gain insights into different functions and promotes a holistic understanding of the business.

19. Regular Performance Reviews: Include collaborative efforts in performance reviews. Recognize and evaluate contributions to cross-departmental projects as part of individual performance assessments.

20. Adaptability: Encourage adaptability to change. In the dynamic business environment, the ability to quickly adapt to new challenges and opportunities is crucial for effective collaboration across departments.

18

Building and maintaining strong relationships with clients in digital marketing:

For building and maintaining strong relationships with clients in digital marketing:

1. Clear Communication: Establish clear and open lines of communication with clients. Regularly update them on project progress, discuss expectations, and address any concerns promptly.

2. Active Listening: Practice active listening to understand your clients' needs, goals, and challenges. This helps build trust and ensures that your strategies align with their objectives.

3. Set Realistic Expectations: Be transparent about what can be achieved within the given timeframe and budget. Setting realistic expectations from the beginning fosters trust and avoids disappointments.

4. Regular Reporting: Provide regular and comprehensive reporting on key performance indicators (KPIs). Clearly showcase the impact of your digital marketing efforts and demonstrate the value you're delivering.

5. Proactive Problem-Solving: Anticipate challenges and proactively address them. Being proactive in problem-solving demonstrates your commitment to the client's success and builds confidence.

6. Personalized Approach: Tailor your approach to each client's unique needs. A personalized strategy shows that you understand their business and are dedicated to achieving results specific to them.

7. Educate Clients: Educate clients about the digital marketing processes and strategies you're employing. This helps them understand the value of your services and fosters a collaborative relationship.

8. Responsive Communication: Respond to client inquiries and messages promptly. Timely communication builds trust and reassures clients that their concerns are a priority.

9. Regular Check-Ins: Schedule regular check-in meetings to discuss progress, address any concerns, and gather feedback. This ongoing dialogue strengthens your client relationships.

10. Client Feedback Surveys: Implement client feedback surveys to gather insights on their satisfaction and areas for improvement. Use this feedback to refine your approach and enhance client satisfaction.

11. Adapt to Client Preferences: Understand and adapt to your clients' communication preferences. Whether they prefer emails, calls, or meetings, accommodating their preferences enhances the client experience.

12. Transparency in Processes: Be transparent about your processes, methodologies, and the tools you use. This transparency builds trust and helps clients understand the value you bring to their business.

13. Celebrating Milestones: Celebrate achievements and milestones together. Acknowledge successes, whether

they're small victories or significant accomplishments, to strengthen the positive aspects of your relationship.

14. Client Collaboration: Foster a collaborative working relationship. Involve clients in decision-making processes and seek their input on key aspects of your digital marketing strategies.

15. Dedicated Account Managers: Assign dedicated account managers or points of contact for clients. Having a consistent contact person helps streamline communication and ensures continuity in the relationship.

16. Surprise and Delight: Occasionally surprise clients with unexpected value. This could be in the form of bonus services, exclusive insights, or special promotions that demonstrate your commitment to their success.

17. Clear Contract Agreements: Ensure that contract agreements are clear, detailed, and mutually agreed upon. This helps prevent misunderstandings and sets the foundation for a strong working relationship.

18. Client Empowerment: Empower clients with knowledge and insights. Provide educational resources, industry trends,

and relevant information that can contribute to their understanding of digital marketing.

19. Accessibility: Be accessible to your clients. Availability and responsiveness contribute to a positive client experience, especially during critical moments or campaigns.

20. Post-Campaign Analysis: Conduct post-campaign analyses to review the performance of digital marketing campaigns. Share insights and recommendations for future strategies, demonstrating your commitment to continuous improvement.

19

Ensuring ethical practices in digital marketing:

For ensuring ethical practices in digital marketing:

1. Adherence to Privacy Regulations: Stay informed and comply with data protection and privacy regulations such as GDPR, CCPA, or other applicable laws. Respect user privacy and obtain explicit consent for data collection and processing.

2. Transparent Data Collection: Clearly communicate to users the purpose and extent of data collection. Provide transparent information about how their data will be used and give them control over their preferences.

3. Honest Advertising: Avoid deceptive or misleading advertising practices. Ensure that your advertisements

provide accurate information about products or services and do not mislead consumers.

4. Authentic Testimonials and Reviews: Use genuine testimonials and reviews. Fabricating or exaggerating customer feedback can damage trust and reputation. Authenticity is crucial in building lasting relationships.

5. Inclusive Marketing: Embrace diversity and inclusion in your marketing efforts. Represent diverse communities, cultures, and perspectives in your content, avoiding stereotypes or discriminatory practices.

6. Responsible Social Media Engagement: Be responsible in your social media engagement. Avoid engaging in practices like fake reviews or fake followers. Focus on building genuine connections with your audience.

7. Respectful Email Marketing: Practice responsible email marketing by obtaining consent before sending promotional emails. Include clear unsubscribe options and respect users' preferences regarding email frequency.

8. Avoid Black-Hat SEO Practices: Stay away from unethical SEO practices that violate search engine guidelines. This includes keyword stuffing, cloaking, or engaging in link

schemes. Focus on creating valuable content and following best practices.

9. Responsible Affiliate Marketing: If using affiliate marketing, ensure that affiliates adhere to ethical standards. Avoid tactics that may harm your brand reputation, and regularly monitor affiliate activities.

10. Customer Data Security: Prioritize the security of customer data. Implement robust security measures to protect sensitive information from unauthorized access or breaches.

11. Social Responsibility Initiatives: Incorporate social responsibility initiatives in your marketing strategies. This could involve supporting charitable causes, promoting sustainability, or contributing to community well-being.

12. Educational Content on Digital Literacy: Provide educational content to promote digital literacy. Help users understand how digital marketing works, recognize online scams, and make informed decisions about their online activities.

13. Responsible Content Creation: Create content that is informative, respectful, and aligns with ethical standards.

Avoid sensationalism, fake news, or content that may spread misinformation.

14. Community Engagement: Engage with your community responsibly. Actively listen to feedback, address concerns, and contribute positively to online discussions, fostering a healthy online environment.

15. Respect Copyright and Intellectual Property: Ensure that your marketing materials respect copyright laws and intellectual property rights. Obtain proper permissions for the use of third-party content and give credit when necessary.

16. Accessibility Considerations: Design your digital content with accessibility in mind. Ensure that your website, apps, and other digital assets are accessible to individuals with disabilities, following accessibility standards.

17. Anti-Discrimination Policies: Implement and adhere to anti-discrimination policies. Ensure that your marketing materials do not discriminate based on race, gender, ethnicity, or any other protected characteristic.

18. Responsible Influencer Partnerships: If engaging with influencers, ensure they align with your brand values. Avoid

partnerships with influencers involved in unethical practices or controversies that may harm your brand.

19. Regular Compliance Audits: Conduct regular audits to ensure ongoing compliance with ethical standards and legal requirements. Stay proactive in identifying and addressing any areas of concern.

20. Employee Training: Train your employees on ethical marketing practices. Ensure that your team is aware of industry guidelines, legal requirements, and the importance of ethical conduct in all marketing activities.

20

Incorporating emerging technologies responsibly in digital marketing:

For Incorporating emerging technologies responsibly in digital marketing:

1. Stay Informed: Keep abreast of the latest emerging technologies relevant to digital marketing. Stay informed through industry publications, conferences, and networking with tech experts.

2. Understand User Privacy: Prioritize user privacy when implementing emerging technologies. Be transparent about data collection, processing, and storage, and comply with privacy regulations.

3. Ethical AI Use: If integrating artificial intelligence (AI), ensure ethical use. Avoid biases, be transparent about AI decision-making, and regularly audit AI systems to identify and rectify any ethical concerns.

4. Responsible Use of Big Data: Utilize big data responsibly. Ensure the ethical collection, storage, and analysis of large datasets, respecting user consent and privacy throughout the process.

5. Accessibility Considerations: Implement emerging technologies with accessibility in mind. Ensure that technology solutions are inclusive and accessible to individuals with disabilities.

6. User Education: Educate users about the technologies you're implementing. Provide clear information on how these technologies enhance their experience and address potential concerns.

7. Feedback Mechanisms: Establish feedback mechanisms for users to express concerns or provide input on the technologies you're implementing. Use this feedback to make improvements and address user needs.

8. Transparency in Automation: If using automation tools, be transparent about their use. Clearly communicate when interactions are automated, and ensure there are mechanisms for users to reach a human representative if needed.

9. Data Security Measures: Implement robust data security measures. Protect sensitive information from unauthorized access, and regularly update security protocols to address evolving threats.

10. Human Oversight: Incorporate human oversight in technology-driven processes. While automation is powerful, having human oversight ensures accountability and addresses situations that may require human judgment.

11. Responsible Chatbots: If using chatbots or conversational AI, design them responsibly. Ensure they provide accurate information, respect user privacy, and seamlessly transition to human support when necessary.

12. Environmental Considerations: Be mindful of the environmental impact of emerging technologies. Explore sustainable options and contribute to reducing the carbon footprint associated with technology use.

13. Responsible VR/AR Implementation: If utilizing virtual or augmented reality, implement these technologies responsibly. Provide clear guidelines for user interaction, prioritize safety, and consider potential physical and mental health impacts.

14. Informed Consent: Obtain informed consent from users before implementing technologies that may collect personal data or track user behavior. Clearly communicate the benefits and potential risks.

15. Ethical Use of Biometrics: If incorporating biometric technologies, prioritize ethical use. Clearly communicate how biometric data is collected, stored, and utilized, and obtain explicit consent from users.

16. Regular Audits and Assessments: Conduct regular audits and assessments of the technologies you've implemented. Evaluate their impact on users, assess for potential biases, and address any issues identified.

17. Collaboration with Ethical Tech Experts: Collaborate with experts in ethical technology to ensure responsible implementation. Seek guidance from professionals who specialize in ethics, privacy, and responsible tech use.

18. Community Engagement: Engage with your community to understand their perspectives on the technologies you're implementing. Be open to feedback and incorporate community input into decision-making.

19. Legal and Ethical Compliance: Ensure that your use of emerging technologies complies with legal and ethical standards. Stay updated on relevant regulations and industry guidelines to maintain compliance.

20. Continuous Learning: Embrace a culture of continuous learning. Stay open to adapting your approach based on new information, user feedback, and evolving ethical considerations in the dynamic landscape of emerging technologies.